797,885 Books
are available to read at

Forgotten Books

www.ForgottenBooks.com

Forgotten Books' App
Available for mobile, tablet & eReader

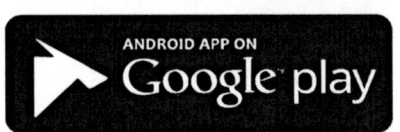

ISBN 978-1-332-99557-8
PIBN 10447729

This book is a reproduction of an important historical work. Forgotten Books uses
state-of-the-art technology to digitally reconstruct the work, preserving the original format
whilst repairing imperfections present in the aged copy. In rare cases, an imperfection in
the original, such as a blemish or missing page, may be replicated in our edition. We do,
however, repair the vast majority of imperfections successfully; any imperfections that
remain are intentionally left to preserve the state of such historical works.

Forgotten Books is a registered trademark of FB &c Ltd.
Copyright © 2015 FB &c Ltd.
FB &c Ltd, Dalton House, 60 Windsor Avenue, London, SW19 2RR.
Company number 08720141. Registered in England and Wales.

For support please visit www.forgottenbooks.com

1 MONTH OF FREE READING

at
www.ForgottenBooks.com

By purchasing this book you are eligible for one month membership to ForgottenBooks.com, giving you unlimited access to our entire collection of over 700,000 titles via our web site and mobile apps.

To claim your free month visit: www.forgottenbooks.com/free447729

* Offer is valid for 45 days from date of purchase. Terms and conditions apply.

English
Français
Deutsche
Italiano
Español
Português

www.forgottenbooks.com

Mythology Photography **Fiction**
Fishing Christianity **Art** Cooking
Essays Buddhism Freemasonry
Medicine **Biology** Music **Ancient Egypt** Evolution Carpentry Physics
Dance Geology **Mathematics** Fitness
Shakespeare **Folklore** Yoga Marketing
Confidence Immortality Biographies
Poetry **Psychology** Witchcraft
Electronics Chemistry History **Law**
Accounting **Philosophy** Anthropology
Alchemy Drama Quantum Mechanics
Atheism Sexual Health **Ancient History**
Entrepreneurship Languages Sport
Paleontology Needlework Islam
Metaphysics Investment Archaeology
Parenting Statistics Criminology
Motivational

TO

HER MOST GRACIOUS MAJESTY

BY THE GRACE OF GOD

QUEEN OF GREAT BRITAIN AND IRELAND
AND EMPRESS OF INDIA

THIS REPRODUCTION

HE FIRST LITERARY EFFORT OF HER ROYAL PREDEC

QUEEN ELIZABETH

IS IN THE

SIXTIETH YEAR

ER MAJESTY'S ILLUSTRIOUS AND BENEFICENT REIGN

A HAPPY PEOPLE,

WITH HER MAJESTY'S GRACIOUS PERMISSION,

DEDICATED

BY HER MOST OBEDIENT HUMBLE SERVANT

THE EDITOR.

5

BADGE OF ANNE BOLEYN, ADOPTED BY THE PRINCESS ELIZABETH
AND RETAINED BY HER AFTER BECOMING QUEEN

ns pas la peine de faire un commentaire.
5

PREFACE

FEW words are needed in explanation of this publication Dr Furnivall, of the Early English Text Society, having called my attention to the original manuscript which lies at the Bodleian, the suggestion to reproduce it was considered by the Council of the Royal Society of Literature, and the appearance of this volume is in consequence of their favorable decision. If the question of literary merit alone had been considered, the publication would scarcely be justified. The 'Miroir' is not the best of the religious poems of Margaret of Navarre, which, with the exception of the 'Chansons Spirituelles,' are inferior to her secular pieces; and a juvenile translation of a poem, admittedly not of high rank, cannot be expected to delight by its intrinsic merits. But the personality of the translator and the circumstances of its production invest the manuscript with peculiar interest. Until eclipsed by the still brighter glories of the reign of our own beloved Sovereign, that of the hitherto peerless Elizabeth stood conspicuously forth as the most splendid that had ever distinguished this nation, and it was naturally thought that the publication of any writing which brought us into closer touch with the mind of Glorious Queen Bess, at any period of her life, would be generally regarded as of value and importance.

It is evident that the manuscript was written by the Princess Elizabeth's own hand, both from a comparison with other specimens of her writing at the same age in the British Museum, notably the autograph book of prayers presented to King Henry, and also from what she says in the dedication. After asking her stepmother to "rubbe out, polishe and mende (or els cause to mende) the wordes (or rather the order of my writting) the wich i knowe in many places to be rude," &c., she expresses the hope that " in the meane whyle no other (but your highnes only) shal rede it or se it lesse my fauttes be knowen of many."

A fac-simile of a letter from the Princess to her brother is given in this volume (following the Introduction) as a specimen of her beautiful writing at a later date

The title of the poem may have been suggested by "Speculum aureum peccatorum," which was "translated at parice oute of laten into frenche," and rendered into English as 'The Mirroure of Golde to the Synfull Soule,' by Margaret, "moder to our Soverain lorde Kinge Henry the VII, and Countess of Rich mond and Derby" This translation, which was imprinted in black letter by Wynken de Worde in 1522, does not give the impression that the original could have contributed any ideas other than the title to Queen Margaret for her 'Miroir de l'âme pécheresse.'

The photogravure frontispiece requires some notice. From the circumstance that only very few of Queen Elizabeth's portraits are dated or signed by the painter, it is necessary to use much care in selecting a portrait which may be regarded as authentic. For the present volume an interesting picture was photographed and printed, but afterwards rejected. It had been supposed to be a portrait of Elizabeth at a very early age, and indeed bears, on a plate, the description "Queen Elizabeth, by Holbein," and is so described in the catalogue of St. James's Palace, where the picture now hangs in the Queen Anne Room; but as the date 1594 appears on the front near the top, there is an evident mistake in the official description. The portrait finally selected and here reproduced presents no difficulties, since it was described in the Catalogues of Kings Henry VIII and Edward VI as "The Ladye Elizabeth her grace, with a booke in her hande, her gowne like crymeson clothe of golde with workes" It is also described as "Queen Elizabeth when young, by H. Holbein," in the Catalogues of Charles I, James II, and Queen Caroline. The official description is as follows:—"Small life-size standing portrait, half-length to the knees. The face to her right, the light from her right side. She has on a red gown cut square across the bosom, and under it a rich gold embroidered petticoat, with long slashed sleeves and small plaited linen ruffs over the hands. Her hands hang down holding a book. She has on a pearl necklace twice round the neck, from which hangs a jewel with three pearls, and at her bosom a larger jewel, on which is a cross of cut stones and three pearls; her fair hair is covered with a red head-dress edged with pearls. Beside her on her right, on a high table, is an open book. Curtains behind the figure. Size of picture, 2 ft. 3 in. by 3 ft. 1½ in., on an oak panel of five pieces dovetailed together."

As Holbein died of the plague in 1543,[1] when the Princess was ten years of age, he cannot possibly have painted this portrait, although it has been attributed to him for 250 years. It was probably painted in 1547 by the same talented but unknown artist who painted the fine portrait of King Edward VI, which is also at Windsor Castle. The delicate hands of Elizabeth, of which she is said to have been rather vain, are well shown in this picture. In face she bears some resemblance to her mother, but she has a more pleasing appearance than Anne Boleyn, and also than her half-sister Mary; but of the children of King Henry VIII, it is only Edward who really had the gift of beauty.

The face of Elizabeth in the original

[1] This fact was established by the late W H. Black, F.S.A. See 'Archæologia,' xxxix, 273.

picture, which is a very fine painting, looks younger than in the plate, and quite reconciles the observer to the generally accepted opinion that the Princess at the time was not more than 13 or 14 years of age, notwithstanding the different impression at first conveyed by the costume and head-dress. The serious expression seems to be the natural effect of an early acquired habit of self-restraint [1]

The prayer, copied by another hand on folio 63 of the manuscript, was composed by Queen Elizabeth for her Navy in 1597, and is the third of " Three most excellent Prayers made by the late famous Queene Elizabeth," published in a quaint volume, 12mo, entitled 'Supplications of Saints, by Tho. Sorocold,

---

[1] In 'Archæologia,' xl, 85, the late Sir G. Scharf, F.S.A., says, with reference to this picture, " The colour of the hair, the set of features, with nose tending to aquiline, and the very slender fingers, all accord with the physique that characterized Elizabeth in after years. Moreover, traces of writing with the name Elizabeth may be observed in the upper left-hand corner."

London   Printed by I. L for H Overton, and are to bee sold at his Shop at the entrance in of Pope's head Alley out of Lombard Street, 1462' (probably intended for 1642).

P. W. A.

20 HANOVER SQUARE W.
  March 1897.

INTRODUCTION

THIS translation, made by Queen Elizabeth during her early childhood (which is in some respects the most attractive period of her life), constitutes an interesting illustration of her precocious ability. It is rather remarkable that this, her first literary work, should have received so little attention. It is not even mentioned by the majority of her numerous biographers, and in Strickland's 'Lives of the Queens of England,' it is incorrectly referred to as "her elegant translation from the Italian"[1]

It was "imprented in the yeare of our lorde 1548, in Apryll," by John Bale, in a volume 12mo under a title of his own as "A Godly Medytacyon of the Christen sowle concerninge a love towardes God and hys Christe."

Elizabeth herself, curiously enough,

[1] Vol. iii, p. 12.

omits to name the distinguished writer of the poem, and neither the title nor the character of the original composition in the French is noticed by Bale. English readers are probably little aware of the fact that the author of the 'Heptameron' was a poet. The novels of the Seven Days, which she partly collected and partly wrote, have been translated, but with the exception of a few lines from the 'Miroir,' and the 'Discord de l'esprit et de la chair,' given in English verse by Dr. H. White, the translator of the first three volumes of the 'History of the Reformation,' by D'Aubigné, and a few casual references elsewhere, the poems have been unnoticed. Queen Margaret's own countrymen were under the like disadvantage until quite recently; for although there had been some new editions, within the last half-century, of 'Les Marguerites,' a considerable part of her poetic work remained entirely unknown until last year.[1]

[1] 'Les Dernières poésies de Marguerite de Navarre,

The translation was undertaken during one of the many clouded periods of Elizabeth's youth. Some time in the year 1543 the little Princess had the misfortune to fall into disgrace at Court, and her royal father's displeasure occasioned her banishment for an entire year, during which time, as she mentions herself, she "had not dared to write to him" In the summer of 1544 King Henry went to Boulogne, and Elizabeth, on being informed that her step-mother, Queen Katherine Parr, had remembered her every time she had written to the King, wrote to her one of her earliest letters thanking the Queen, and beseeching her to recommend her to His Majesty, praying for his sweet benediction[1] Shortly afterwards, in September, the King intimated his forgiveness in a general blessing to all his children,

publiées pour la première fois, avec une introduction et des notes par Abel Lefranc, Secrétaire du Collège de France,' Paris, 1896.

[1] The original letter, written in Italian, is in the Bodleian.

and at the close of that year Elizabeth sent her translation, in all probability bound with her own hands,[1] as a New Year's gift to the Queen. It may, therefore, be regarded as an offering of grateful affection.

The translation and the letter naturally direct attention to her early accomplishments, for even supposing that Castiglione, her Italian master, may have been in part responsible for the latter,

[1] In the centre of each cover are the Queen's initials, K. P., and in each corner a heart's-ease. (For instances of the use of the device of a pansy flower as an ornament about the time, see 'Archæologia,' xxxix, 270, 271.) The design, which is the same on both sides, is worked in gold and silver wire on a ground of blue corded silk. On the back there are four panels with an embroidered flower in each. The edges are bound with gold braid, with a narrow line of red silk at the top and bottom. The Princess also bound and embroidered a beautiful autograph book of prayers, now preserved in the British Museum. It is dedicated as follows:—"Illustrissimo Henrico octavo Anglie, Francie, Hibernieq. regi, fidei defensori," &c. In the centre of the cover she has made a monogram of these titles of the king, with the letter H. at the top and at the bottom, and in each corner a rose. It appears to be worked with red silk and gold wire, with green leaves in silk. (See 'Early English Embroidered Books,' by Cyril James Davenport, London, 1888.)

Embroidered Cover of the original Manuscript of

"THE MIROIR OR GLASSE OF THE SYNNEFULLE SOULE,"

Worked by the Princess Elizabeth when Eleven Years of Age.

SIZE $7\frac{3}{8} \times 5\frac{1}{2}$ in.

yet there exists too much independent evidence of her easy familiarity with languages to doubt her linguistic skill. All contemporary accounts agree in attributing to her a love of study and a quickness of apprehension French, Italian, Spanish, and Flemish she both wrote and spoke with facility, and Miss Strickland says she astonished some of the most erudite linguists of that age by the ease and grace with which she conversed in the Latin tongue.

Heywood thus writes with reference to Elizabeth and Edward, who for a very happy period of their youth studied together:—" So ingenious were either, that they desired to looke upon bookes as soone as the day began to breake their *horæ matutinæ* were so welcome that they seemed to prevent the nights sleeping for the entertainment of the morrows schooling · and when hee was cal'd out to any youthfull exercise becomming a child of his age, . . . she in her private Chamber betook herselfe to her Lute or violl and (wearied with that) to practise her needle."[1] Hentzner, the German traveller, mentions having seen a little volume in the royal library at Whitehall, written on vellum in French by Queen Elizabeth when a child. It was thus inscribed:—"A tres haut, et tres puissant, et redoubté prince Henry, VIII de ce nom, roy d'Angleterre, de France, et de Irelande, defenseur de la foy, Elisabeth, sa tres humble fille, rend salut et obédience." There are two interesting references to the Princess when she was six years of age. One is recorded in "Ellis's Royal Letters," and states that "on the second anniversary of Edward's birth, when the Nobles of England presented gifts of silver and gold and jewels to the infant heir of the realm, the lady Elizabeth's grace gave the simple offering of a shirt of cambric, worked by her own hands." The other is made by Wriothesley, who

[1] 'England's Elizabeth,' by Tho. Heywood, London, 1631.

visited Elizabeth at Hertford Castle on December 17th, 1539. He writes, "I then went to my lady Elizabeth's grace, and to the same made His Majesty's most hearty commendations, declaring that his Highness desired to hear of her health, and sent his blessing; she gave humble thanks, inquiring after His Majesty's welfare, and that with as great a gravity as if she had been forty years old." It is natural to expect in the history of her childhood some evidence of those intellectual gifts which made her the most learned woman of her age, and one of its keenest politicians; but it is pleasant to find also conclusive proofs of a sweetness of disposition which made her beloved by all who knew her, which elicited expressions of devoted attachment from her brother, and softened the natural antipathy of the injured Princess Mary. The latter's generous championship of her little sister forms one of many illustrations of the fine character and amiable natural disposition of that

Princess, as displayed in her earlier years. She deliberately defied the orders of Council degrading her sister's rank, by persistently giving her the title of *grace;* and at the time when King Henry had just disowned the daughter of Anne Boleyn, Mary courageously recommended her to his favorable notice in a letter addressed directly to the king. It is dated from Hunsdon, July 21st (1536). The concluding paragraph is as follows — "My sister Elizabeth is in good health (thanks to our Lord), and such a child toward, as I doubt not but your Highness shall have cause to rejoice of in time coming (as knoweth Almighty God), who send your Grace, with the Queen my good mother, health, with the accomplishment of your desires" Leti[1] tells us that when Anne of Cleves saw Elizabeth she was charmed with her beauty, wit, and endearing caresses, and conceived the most tender affection for her; and when the conditions of the

[1] Quoted by Strickland.

divorce were arranged she requested as a great favour that she might be permitted to see her sometimes, adding "that to have had that young Princess for her daughter would have been greater happiness to her than being Queen." Lady Bryan, her first governess, speaks of her docility and gentleness in a letter to Sir T. Cromwell. Most agreeable evidence of Elizabeth's affectionate disposition is found in her relations with her brother Edward. It appears that she undertook the pleasant task of giving the first lessons to her infant brother, for, says Heywood, "shee was 3 yeares elder then her Brother, and therefore able in her pretty language to teach and direct him (even fro the first of his speech and understanding)"[1] The sentiments of the young Prince are shown in his letters, of which one written when he was nine years of age after their separation was as follows:—

[1] Elizabeth was born on September 7th, 1533, and Edward on October 12th, 1537. She was therefore four years older than her brother.

"The change of place, most dear sister, does not so much vex me as your departure from me. But nothing can now occur to me more grateful than your letters. I particularly feel this, because you first began the correspondence, and challenged me to write to you I thank you most cordially both for your kindness and the quickness of its coming, and I will at least equal you in regard and attention. It is a comfort to my regret, that I hope shortly to see you again if no accident intervenes." In the first letter which he wrote to her after he became King, in answer to one of condolence from her on the subject of their common bereavement, he again addresses her as his "sweetest sister," and refers to her learning and prudence which enable her to know what to do, and which relieve him from the necessity of consoling her; and after complimenting her upon her elegant sentences, he observes that she thinks of their father's death with a calm mind. This was no doubt written in all simplicity, but, considering the continual terror that cruel father must have been to his sister, it can scarcely be regarded as an instance of fortitude that she bore his removal calmly. The letter was written in Latin, and the sentences referred to are as follows :—" Minimi opus est mihi te consolari, charissima soror, quod eruditione tua cognoscis quid sit faciendum, prudentia vero et pietate tua quod eruditio docuit te cognoscere facto præstas. . . . Præterea literæ tuæ mihi admodum arridebant, tum quod in illis elegantes sententiæ continentur, tum quod ex illis sentio te æquo consuluisse animo mortem patris nostri."[1]

No one can study the early lives of Mary, Elizabeth, and Edward without quickly perceiving that they were very remarkable children   Their qualities and attainments are attributable partly to inheritance and partly to the educative

[1] 'Original Letters Illustrative of English History,' with notes and illustrations by Henry Ellis, F.R.S., London, 1824.

influence of the altogether exceptional circumstances in which they were placed Pride, fearlessness, a high spirit, and a strong will were possessed by all members of the House of Tudor, and they all likewise displayed in different degrees a prudence and discretion which averted at the last moment the dangers which their obstinacy frequently gathered about them Their faults as well as their merits were exhibited by Elizabeth, who excelled them all, however, in diplomatic skill and intelligence. Her letters and her "golden speeches" reveal a style admirable in temper, dignity, and grace, and her expressions of the trust and affection in which she held her people never failed to touch their hearts and to arouse their enthusiastic loyalty and devotion This was especially noticeable in those critical conflicts which occasionally arose between the Crown and the Commons, when, as Macaulay says, "she left to her successors a memorable example of the way in which it behoves a ruler to deal with public movements which he has not the means of resisting." An element of greatness in the character of Elizabeth is that robust independence of mind which enabled her to remain uninfluenced by the delusive appearances and conventional distinctions which affect the opinions and actions of ordinary men and women. For many years she succeeded in suppressing the persecuting spirit and skilfully held the balance of opposing creeds. It was this intellectual detachment which enabled her to initiate a policy so wise, temperate and beneficent, as to secure her the devotion of her subjects. "She saw that to make a government flourish there must be internal peace and security, and that its councillors must be men of ability and virtue" (Buckle). Her many royal qualities have at all times inclined men to ignore her faults, and even those who suffered from them cannot withhold their tribute of praise. Neal, in his 'History of the Puritans,' after censuring the cruelty with which she treated men of Puritan opinions, concludes, "However, notwithstanding all these blemishes, Queen Elizabeth stands upon record as a wise and politic Princess. She was the glory of the age in which she lived, and will be the admiration of posterity."[1] But the students of that glorious epoch, and the admirers of its brilliant central figure, are unable to include in their laudations the moral side of that interesting character. Even after allowances are justly made for the peculiarities of the time, for the general acceptance and recognition of diplomatic mendacity as an "intellectual means of meeting a difficulty," there yet remains the conspicuous absence of the gentler and purer qualities of womanhood. It was left for a happier age to experience, in a still more glorious reign, the felicitous union of a noble wisdom with a pure morality

[1] 'The History of the Puritans,' by Daniel Neal, M.A., second edition, corrected, London, 1754, vol. i, p. 403.

Some examination of the methods of the education of this great Princess may be of interest. As was usual at that time with young students, she was accustomed to long hours and hard reading. The list of subjects included in the studies of the royal children astonishes us by its character and variety. In the 'Chronicle' of Crispin it is related that the Princess Mary studied astronomy, geography, natural philosophy, and mathematics; that she read the orators, the historians, and the poets of Greece and Rome in their native languages. Needlework and music were also assiduously practised.

Hayward gives the following pleasant description of the boy king Edward:—
"He attained not only commendable knowledge but speech in the Greeke, Spanish, and Italian languages having alwaies great judgement in measuring his words by his matter; his speech being alike both fluent and weightie, such as best beseemed a Prince. As for naturall

Philosophie, Logicke, Musicke, Astronomie, and other liberall sciences, his perfections were such that the great Italian philosopher Cardane, having tasted him most strongly to encounter his new devised paradoxes in Philosophie, seemed to be astonished betweene admiration and delight, ... in disposition he was mild, gracious and pleasant in body beautifull, but especially in his eies which seemed to have a starrie livelinesse and lustre in them generally he seemed to be as Cardane reported of him, a Miracle of Nature."[1]

Reference has already been made to the avidity with which Elizabeth and Edward called for their books "as soon as the day began to breake," and Heywood further records that "the rest of the forenoon (breakfast-time excepted) they were instructed in language, or some of the liberal sciences, or moral learning, collected out of such authors as did best

[1] 'The Life and Reigne of King Edward the Sixth,' by Sir John Hayward, London, 1636.

conduce to the instruction of princes." Of the genuineness of this study the Queen gave many interesting proofs in later life, as for instance when, without hesitation or previous preparation, she answered in one day three Ambassadors each in his own language; and again on the occasion of her visit to Oxford she delivered an oration in Latin We read of the same long hours and extensive list of subjects studied, in the early history of Margaret of Navarre, the Lady Jane Grey, and others, yet we do not hear of any of these industrious students suffering from "over-pressure." The modern system of "working for examinations," with the inevitable introduction of that brain-destructive element of *anxiety* into the studies of the young, was then happily unknown. Free from this false ambition they were able to acquire a disinterested love of knowledge, and to appreciate the worth and delight of intellectual effort for its own sake, with the result that their minds attained a degree of clearness, alacrity, and vigour otherwise unattainable There is another point worthy of consideration. There are two theories of education, based upon principles whose operations have been exhibited not only in every special legislative effort to provide for the instruction of the young, but also in all the great intellectual conflicts and controversies out of which modern civilisation has evolved. In the one is to be observed the solicitude of the preceptor to form, control, and direct the mind of the pupil, to furnish knowledge of the wisdom of the past, to develop veneration for constituted authority, to create mistrust of self in forming judgments and opinions. In the other there is to be seen an effort to remove every obstacle to the natural expansion of the mind, to promote the growth and development of all the faculties, to furnish materials for the formation of independent judgment, and to encourage its exercise. These theories when thus stated appear to be mutually opposed, but they should be complementary to each other. Just as the well-being of a state depends on the great principles of order and progress, so in the development of the human mind the steadying influence of discipline is no less essential than the moving power of unimpeded growth. The education of the Princess Elizabeth, rather by the force of circumstances than by the conscious intention of her tutors, approximated to the latter scheme. The periods of neglect with which the vicissitudes of her youth were marked left her in freedom to follow the direction of her natural tastes, and she, no doubt, interpreted for herself the lessons of history, her favourite subject. By this unrestrained study and reflection she was able to cultivate her intellect to its loftiest extent, and to develop her natural strength of character to an astonishing degree of self-reliance.

The omission of the Princess to name

the author of the 'Mirror' when she mentions that poem in her dedication to Queen Katherine Parr, conveys the idea that she probably knew little or nothing of Marguerite d'Angoulême, and that there could not have been any connecting links in their respective histories. As there are several circumstances which should have made the name of the Queen of Navarre familiar, if this ignorance is a correct surmise, the true explanation lies in the pathetic fact that this bright and lovable child never knew anything of home-life or the delight of a mother's tales of bygone times. Anne Boleyn's unhappy end came when her daughter was only three years old, and the history of that brief period is unrelieved by any accounts of motherly care and affection. Had it been otherwise, Elizabeth might have heard much of the gifted lady whose poem had attracted her attention and stirred her childish ambition to render it into English. For Anne Boleyn, who had accompanied King Henry's sister, Mary Tudor, to France after the latter's marriage by proxy with Louis XII, remained there when the death of that monarch terminated the brief union, and after a short period at the court of Claude, Queen of Francis I, she entered the service of Margaret, who was then Duchesse d'Alençon, and therefore we may conclude that the copy of 'Miroir de l'âme pécheresse' in Elizabeth's possession, had belonged to her mother, who may have obtained it from her former friend and mistress. Margaret might have become much more closely associated with the English royal house if certain negotiations had been attended with success, for after the death of Elizabeth of York in 1503, at which time Margaret was 12 years of age, Henry VII became a suitor for her hand in marriage. This was not the only escape she had from the doubtful privilege of being allied to the House of Tudor, for when Henry VIII first entertained the idea of divorcing Katherine of Arragon he also opened negotiations with Margaret, then the widow of the Duke of Alençon. It is said, on rather insufficient authority, that in rejecting this proposal Margaret made to Wolsey, who was conducting the matter, the following spirited reply: "Katherine of Arragon, your injured Queen, was the friend of my dear and gentle sister Queen Claude, and for her sake, if for no other, I should spurn your proposal. But not for worlds would I be accessory to an act of injustice like that which you contemplate; and certainly I could never trust my happiness in the hands of a man who is stained with such a crime."[1] Though we have no proof that Elizabeth when a child knew Margaret, the latter's attention must soon have been drawn to Elizabeth, for the first in the long series of negotiations for the marriage of our Princess took place when she was only 13 months old, at which

[1] 'Margaret, the Pearl of Navarre,' Edinburgh, 1868.

time her father proposed a union with Margaret's nephew, the young Duke of Angoulême, the third son of Francis I

Disregarding these externals there may be found a much more important and significant connection between the author and the translator of the 'Mirror.' Both were completely in sympathy with the great movement of that age, that had for its object to purify and spiritualize the Christian Church; Margaret adopting the principles of her friend Erasmus, Elizabeth, by throwing off the external yoke of the Latin Church, may be regarded as the follower of Luther " Erasmus and Luther," says d'Aubigné " viewed in connexion with the Reformation, are the representatives of two great ideas —of two great parties in their age, and indeed in every age. The one is composed of men of timid prudence, the other of men of resolution and courage."[1] These parties, personified in

[1] 'History of the Reformation,' by J. H. M d'Aubigné, Edinburgh, 1846.

their illustrious chiefs, were represented also in the witty, satirical but timid Margaret, and in the lion-hearted Elizabeth. The dread of unknown troubles following violent changes, which led Erasmus to recommend putting up with ungodly princes,[1] is reflected in Margaret, who never ventured to add reproof to her exhortations to her brother. She resembled the great "Writer of the Opposition" in her methods of exposing error by the popular weapon of sarcasm, but she displayed none of the personal vanity which excited the scorn of his enemies; nor does the student of her life find intermingled with his sympathy with her sorrows, the sense of *disappointment* occasioned by the history of Erasmus. Margaret had neither the authority nor the personal greatness of Elizabeth, and her influence was exercised by the example of her life and by her writings, while she outwardly con-

[1] Præstat ferre principes impios, quam novatis rebus gravius malum accersere.

formed to the orthodox church ; while that of our great Queen was enforced by her army and her navy, and she was the open and avowed champion of the new doctrines, and has been justly regarded as the Nursing Mother of the Reformation. In this sense Elizabeth's life was a continuation and fulfilment of the promise of Margaret's, and it was assisted by the circumstances of the time and by the development of events The two lives coincided in point of time for sixteen years, the closing period of Margaret's career and the opening of Elizabeth's

In studying the life of Margaret we have not to deal with the mighty intellect and profound sagacity of Elizabeth, nor do we meet with the strange incongruities of the latter's character, nor is the group of literary men which attended the *salons* of the Queen of Navarre, giving them the name of the New Parnassus, comparable to the bright constellation of the sons of genius which adorned the court of the English Queen ; yet her history, if less brilliant, is still full of interest "Marguerite humaine, douce et sage," as contemporary poets sang " le pur élixir des Valois," as Michelet described her, was born on the 11th of April, 1492, two years before the birth of her brother Francis. Her parents were Charles, Count of Angoulême, and Louise of Savoy. Her numerous titles are rather bewildering. As a descendant of the royal family of Valois she was known in her girlhood as Margaret of Valois; from the place of her birth and her father's title she obtained the name by which she is best known in history, Marguerite d'Angoulême; in her fifteenth year she married the Duke d'Alençon, and took the titles of Madame and Duchesse d'Alençon; she is also known as Margaret of Orleans, as belonging to the Orleans branch of the Royal House; and as Margaret of Navarre, of which province she was Queen; finally when Francis became King he made his sister

Madame de France. In 1528 she married Henry d'Albret, King of Navarre, who was 11 years her junior, and she died at the castle of Odos, December 21st, 1549, her life thus extending over that of her brother two years at the beginning and at the end. It is rather curious that her first funeral verses, written in Latin, were nominally by Anne, Margaret, and Jane Seymour, nieces of the mother of Edward VI. Margaret's character, and the high estimation in which she was held, are best shown in the recorded opinions of her contemporaries, and her letters to the King, her brother, when he was in captivity in Madrid, leave no doubt in the reader's mind of the sincerity of her religious convictions. Her brother always called her his Darling,[1] the Pearl of Valois, &c., and he is reported to have said on one occasion, "My sister Margaret is the only woman I ever knew who has every virtue and every

[1] 'Vie des Dames illustrés,' La Haye, 1740.

grace without one mixture of vice; and yet she is never wearisome or insipid as you good people are apt to be." Henry II, the successor of Francis, said, "If it were not for my aunt Margaret I should doubt the existence of such a thing as genuine goodness on the earth, but never have I been disappointed in her." Brantôme says, "She chose for her emblem the marigold, which by its rays and leaves has a seeming affinity with the sun, and turns wherever he goes. She added the device 'I seek not things below,'[1] as a sign that she directed all her actions, thoughts, desires, and affections to that great Sun which is God; and hence she was suspected of being attached to the Lutheran religion." He says elsewhere, "Every one loved her, for she was kind to all, gracious, charitable, and affable, a great almsgiver, but withal bestowing words and smiles more precious than gold; despising no one, and winning all hearts by her excel-

[1] Non inferiora secutus.

lent qualities" To those who know Margaret only as the compiler of the 'Heptameron,' such descriptions of her will be very curious as revealing unsuspected qualities in that lively satirist and others less fortunate, to whom the 'Heptameron' is unknown, might form, from the foregoing quotations, a very different picture from the bright, witty, and vivacious reality. From the fact that Margaret at least tolerated the vices of her much-loved brother, and also from the malicious slanders invented by the haters of her heresy, and perhaps from the impressions of careless readers of the 'Heptameron,' a quite erroneous reputation of moral laxity has been associated with her name. But " Un doux nenny avec un doux sourire" is all that her lovers received, which Mr. Saintsbury thinks sufficiently indicates that she was a virtuous coquette if somewhat coquettishly virtuous [1]

[1] Essay by George Saintsbury, included in the edition of the 'Heptameron' printed for the Society of English Bibliophilists, 1894.

'Le Miroir de l'âme pécheresse' is in rhymed decasyllables, and reveals much of the personal religious history of its writer. Other poems somewhat similar are, 'Oraison de l'Ame Fidèle à son Seigneur Dieu,' and 'Le triomphe de l'Agneau,' which is generally considered to be the best.

The address " Au Lecteur," prefacing Le Miroir,' is as follows ·

"Si vous lisez ceste œuvre toute entiere
Arrestez vous, sans plus, à la matiere,
En excusant la rhythme et le language,
Voyant que c'est d'une femme l'ouvrage,
Qui n'a en soy science, ne sçavoir,
Fors un desir, que chacun puisse voir
Que fait le don de Dieu le Createur,
Quand il luy plaist justifier un cœur;
Quel est le cœur d'un homme, quant à soy
Avant qu'il ayt receu le don de Foy,
Par lequel seul l'homme a la congnoissance
De la Bonté, Sapience et Puissance.
Et aussi tost qu'il congnoit Verité,
Son cœur est plein d'Amour et Charité
Ainsi bruslant, perd toute vaine crainte,
Et fermement espere en Dieu sans feinte,
Ainsi le don que liberalement
Le Createur donne au commencement

N'ha nul repos, qu'il n'ayt deïfié
Celuy qui s'est par Foy en Dieu fié,
O l'heureux don, qui fait l'homme Dieu estre
Et posseder son tant desirable Estre.
Helas ! jamais nul ne le peult entendre,
Si par ce don n'a pleu à Dieu le prendre.
Et grand' raison ha celuy d'en douter,
Si Dieu au cœur ne luy a fait gouster,
   Mais vous, Lecteurs de bonne conscience,
Je vous requiers, prenez la patience
Lire du tout ceste œuvre qui n'est rien,
Et n'en prenez seulement que le bien
   Mais priez Dieu, plein de bonté naïve
Qu'en vostre cœur il plante la Foy vive.

The text begins

Où est l'Enfer remply entierement
De tout malheur, travail, peine et tourment ?
Où est le puitz de malediction,
D'où sans fin sort desesperation ?
Est il de mal nul sy profond abysme
Qui suffisant fust pour punir la disme
De mes pechés, qui sont en sy grand nombre
Qu'infinité rend sy obscure l'ombre
Que les compter ne bien voir je ne puys ?
Car trop avant avecques eux je suis.

"The plan of these poems," says Mr. Saintsbury, "is taken from the long-winded allegorical erotic poetry of the very late thirteenth, the fourteenth, and the fifteenth centuries,—poetry which is now the most difficult to read in any literature." Beza says, " 'The Mirror of the Sinful Soul' was composed in a strain very unusual in the Church of Rome, there being no mention made in it either of male or female saints, or of merits, or of any other purgatory than the blood of Jesus Christ." That the heretical tendency of the poem attracted much attention at the time is shown in many ways. The students of the College of Navarre acted a comedy in which Margaret was represented as a Fury of Hell; for which, however, they were afterwards committed to prison. The University of the Sorbonne condemned the book as heretical, and ordered the copies to be burnt, from which fate they were saved by the express intervention of the King. Nicolas Cop, rector of the Sorbonne, expressly disowned the censure pronounced by the body over which he presided; but Noël Bédier, syndic of the faculty of theology, who had been the most ardent promoter of the attacks on Queen Margaret, died in confinement at Mont Saint Michel

At a later time, when Margaret's power to secure protection for herself and her friends was much weaker, Bonaventure Despériers, who was in her service and who had a hand, it is thought, in producing the 'Heptameron,' was driven to suicide by the persecution he received, in 1544, the same year in which Elizabeth rendered the suspected ' Mirror' into English.

The volume already referred to, ' Les Dernières poésies de Marguerite de Navarre,' published in 1896, contains, as its editor, M. Lefranc, says, "together with a number of the most personal and characteristic of her works, the history of the secret of her life. The words contained in these forgotten pages are by turns words of sadness and of hope, but on the whole the sentiment which inspires the essential parts, and above all the conclusion, is that of a bright cheerfulness. It is a song of deliverance and of moral enfranchisement, which is the keynote of these poems. We thus perceive the supreme evolution which is accomplished in that great soul, in the course of the three or four years which preceded and followed the death of Francis I. . . . No other hand appears to have turned the leaves of these precious pages since the day when Jeanne d'Albret enclosed in an iron casket, garnished with solid locks, the manuscript which she wished, by a scruple easy to understand, to conceal from all unsympathetic eyes. . . . She always guarded with a jealous care the collection which she considered as the literary testament of her mother, that which contained the *confessions* of the most lovable of the women of the Renaissance " These poems consist of ten epistles in verse, two comedies, three lyrics, six elegies, and two considerable poems, 'The Prisons of the Queen of Navarre' (her greatest work) and 'The Ship' and they fill 439 pages, 8vo That these interesting poems, revealing as they do so much of the inner life of the gifted Margaret, should have remained entirely neglected and unknown for 350 years is indeed surprising. The thanks of the world of letters are due to Monsieur Abel Lefranc for again awakening the musical voice of the Pearl of Valois

5

Like as a shipman in stormy wether plukes downe the sailes tarijnge for bettar winde, so did I, most noble Kinge, in my vnfortunat chanche thursday pluk downe the hie sailes of my ioy, and do trust one day that as troblesome wanes haue repul me bakwarde, so a gentil winde wil bringe me forwarde to my hauen. Two chief occasions moued me muche and grieued me gretly, the one for that I douted your Maiestie belthe, the other bicause for al my longe tarijnge I wente without that I came for, of the first I am releued in a parte, bothe that I vnderstode of your helthe and also that your Maiesties loginge is far fro my Lorde Marques chamber, of my other grief I am not eased, but the best is that whatsoeuer other folkes wil suspect, I intende not to feare your graces goodwil, wiche as I knowe that I neuer disarued to faint, so I trust wil stil stike by me. For if your graces aduis that I shulde retourne (whos wil is a comandemente) had not bine, I wold not haue made the halfe of my way, the ende of my iourney. And thus as one desirous to hire of your Maiesties helth thoogh vnfortunat to se it I shal pray God for euer to preserue you. From Hatfilde this present saterday.

Your Maiesties humble sister to comandemente, Elizabeth

5

Fol. 1

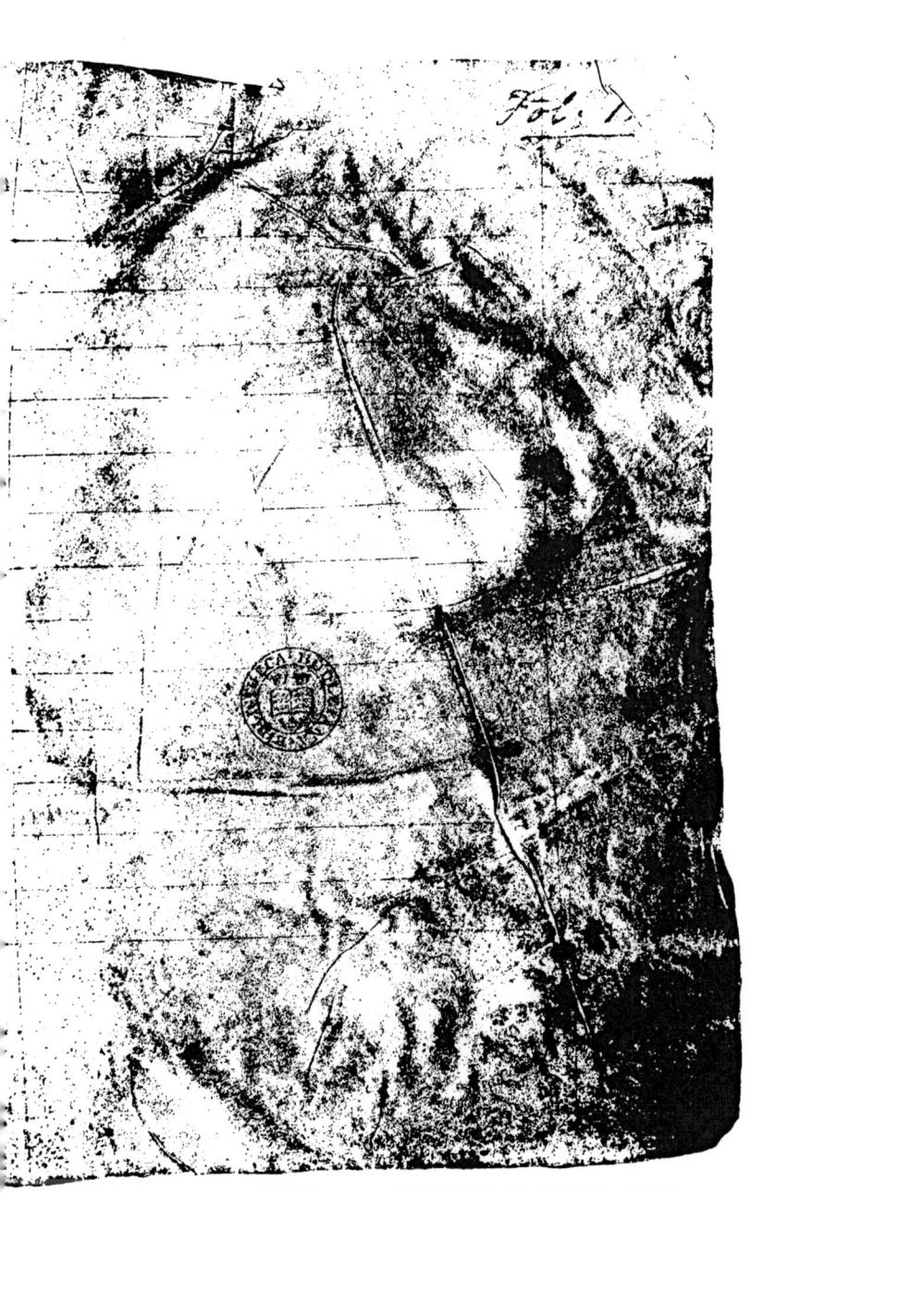

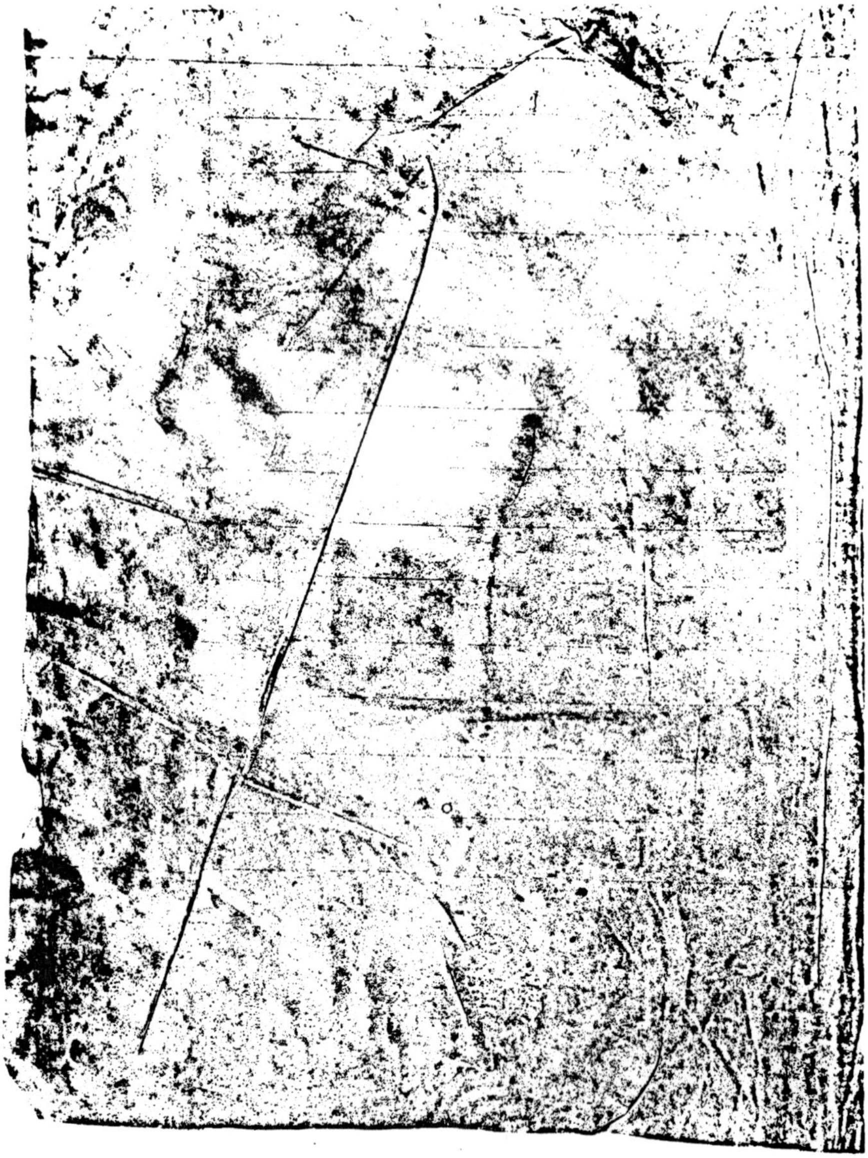

TO OVR MOST NOBLE AND
vertuous quene KATHERIN, Elizabeth her humble daughter wisheth
perpetuall felicitie and euerlasting joye

NOT ONELY knowing the affe-
ctuous wille, and feruent zeale the
which your highnes hath towardes
all godly lerning, as also my duetie
towardes you (most gracious and
souerayne princes) but knowing also that
pusilanimite and yellenes are most
repugnant vnto a reasonable creature: and that (as the philosopher
sayeth) euen as an instrument of yron

or of other mctayle, waxeth soone
musty, or elles be contynualy occupied.
Euen ryght so shall the wytte of a man, or
woman, waxe dull, and vnapte to
do or vnderstand any thing pfitely.
onles it be alwayes occupied in
some maner of study. Whiche thinges
consydered, hath moued so small a
portion, as god hath lente me to
proue what i could do. And therfore
haue, (as for a sere or beginninge) fo
lowing the ryght notable sayeng of the
prouerbe aforesayd) translated this
lytell boke out of frenche ryme in to
englysshe prose, ioyning ỹ sentences

together as well as the capacitie of
my symple witte, and small lerning
coulde extende themselues. The wich
booke is intytled, or named ye mirour
or glasse, of the synnefull soule where
in (it is conteyned, how she (beholdig
and contempling what she is) doth
perceyue how, of herselfe, and of her
owne strenght, she can do nothing
that good is, or preuayleth for her
saluacion: onles it be through the
grace of god. whose mother, daugh
ter, syster, and wife, by ye scriptures
she proueth herselfe to be. Trusting
also, that through his incōprehen

sible loue, grace, and mercy. She (beynge called from synne to repentaunce) doth faythfully hope to be
saued. And althou hei knowe y
as for my parte, wich i haue wrought
in it, that (as well spirituall, as manuall)
there is nothinge done as it shulden
be, nor els worthy to come in youre
graces handes, but rather all vnper-
fytt, and vncorrect: yet do i truste
also that oubeit it is like a worke wich
is but . . . it begonne, and shapen by
the fyle of youre excellent witte, and
godly . . . in the redinge of it (if
so it vouchesafe . . . highnes to do)

shall rubbe out, polishe, and mende
(or els cause to mende) the wordes (or
rather the order of my writtinge) the
wich i knowe in many places to be
rude, and nothinge done as it shuld
be. But i hope, that after to haue ben
in youre graces handes: there shall
be nothinge in it worthy of reprehen
sion, and that in the meane while
no other (but your highnes onely) shal
rede it, or se it, lesse my fauttes be
knowen of many. Than shall they be
better excused (as my confidence is in
youre graces accoustumed beneuolece)
than if i shuld bestowe a whole yere

in writtinge, or inuentinge wayes for
to co[...]m. Prayeng god almigh
[...] and creatoure of all[...]
[...] vnto your high
[...] newe [...] daye, a lucky
[...] perous [...]re, with pros[...]
[...]tye, and continuan[...]
yeres in good helth, and co[...] all
ioy, and all to his honoure, praise, and
glory. From [...]sheri[...]ge, the laste daye
of [...] of the yeare of our lord
[...] god, 1544.

To the reader

IF thou doest rede thys whole w
worke; beholde rather the matter
and occuse the speche, consydering
it is the worke of a woman: wiche
hath in her neyther science, or know
ledge, but a desyre that eche one
might se, what the gifte of god doth
when it pleaseth hym to iustifie the
harte of a man. ffor what thinge is
a man (as for hys owne strenght)
before that he hath receyued the gifte
of fayth: wherby onely, hath ye know
ledge of the goodnes, wysdom, and

power of god, and as soone as he
knoweth the truthe, than is his hart
full of loue, and charitie. so that by
the feruentenes therof he doth exclu
de all vayne feare, and stedfastely
doth hope vpon god vnfaynedly.
Euen so the gifte the wich oure crea
tour giueth at the beginninge doth
neuer reste, tyll he hath made hym
godly, wich putteth hys trust in god
O the hapy gifte wich causeth a mā
to be like vnto god, and to possesse
hys so desyred dwellinge. Alas no
man coulde neuer vnderstande it, on
les by this gifte god hathe gyuen

hym it, and he hath greate cause to
doute of it, onles god hath made hym
selfe it in to hys harte. Wherfore reader
with a godly mynde i beeche beseche
the to take it paciently to peruse this
worke, wich is but lytell, and taste
nothinge but the frutte of it, praieng
to god full of all goodnes, that in
your harte he will plante
the liuely fayth.

THE glasse of the synnefull soule.

Make me a cleane harte O god.

WHERE is the hell full of trauayle
payne, mischiefe, and turmente, where
is the pytte of cursydnes, out of the
wich doth springe all despaire. Is
there any hell so profunde, that is suf-
ficiente to punishe the tenth parte of
my synnes, wich be of so great a number, that the infinite doth make the
shadow so darke, that i can not se
compte them, or els scantly se them.
ffor i am to farre entred emongest

them and that worse is, i haue not y
power to obtayne the true knowled
ge of one. I fele well that the roote of
it is in me, and outwardly i se none
other effect, but all is eyther braun=
che, leaffe, or els frutte that she brin
geth furth all aboute me. If i thinke
to loke for better, a braunche cometh
and doth close myne eyes: and in=
my mouth doth fall when i wolde
speake the frutte wich is so bytter to
swalowe down. If my sprite be styr
red for to harken, than a great mul
titude of leaffes doth entre in myne
eares and my nose is all stoped

with flowres. Now behold how in
paynes, crycnge, and wepinge my
poore soule, a slaue, and prisonnere
doth lye, withoute clartie, or light,
hauinge both her fete bound by her
concupiscence, and also both her
armes through yuell vse; yet y̆ power
to remedy it, doth not lye in me, and
power haue i none, to cry helpe. Now
as ferforth as i can i ought to haue
no hope of succoure; but through y̆
grace of god, wiche i can not deserue,
the wiche maye rayse euery one frō
death. By hys brightenes he gyueth
light to my darkenes, and his power,

examininge my fautte, doth breake
all the vayle of ignorauncy, and geueth
me cleare vnderstanding, not onely
that thys cometh of me, but also what
thinge abydeth in me, where i am
and wherfore i do laboure, who he
is whom i haue offended, to whom
also i did obey so seldom. Therfore
it is conuenient that my pryde be
supressed, and humbly i do confesse
that, as for me, i am muche lesse thā
nothinge: before my byrthe, mer—   iob.10.
and after, a dongehyll. A body redy   and.40.
and prompt to do all yuell, not wil—   genes.
linge other study, also subiette to

care for trub. and payne a shorte
lyfe, and the onde vncertyne the
wich vnderneth by adam is solde
and by the lawe iudged to be hange.
ffor i had neuer the power to obserue onely.
one of the cōmaundementes of god
I do fele the strenght of synne to be
in me: therfore is my synne nowhitt
the lesse to be hydden and y⟨e⟩ more
I dyssembled outwardlly harte so
muche the more he encreasyth within the harte. Thys that god will
i cannot wille: and what he will
not, i oftentimes desyre to haue se⟨e⟩
wich thinges doth constrayne me

by importable sorowe, to wyshe for
the ende of thys myserable life, throug
desyred death, bycause of my wery
and ragyd life. Who shall be he
than that shall delyuer, and recou
uer suche good for me. Alas, it can
not be a mortall man: ffor his power
and strenght is not such: but it
shall be the onely good grace of al
mighty god, wich is neuer slake to
preuente vs with hys mercy. Alas,
what a mayster withoute to haue
serued any goodnes of hym: but ra
ther serued hym sloughtfully, and
withoute cease offended hym euery

daye, yet ys he not slake in helping me
He doth shew yuell that i haue done,
what .... muche it is, and how
of my selfe, i can do nothinge y⟨at is⟩ good
but with harte, and body so enclined
to the contrary, that i fele no strenght
in me, onles it be for to do yuell. He
doth not tary tyll i humbly do
praye hym, or that (seynge my hell
and damnacion) i do cry vpon
hym. ffor, with hys spirite, he doth
make a wyllinge withyne my hart,
greater than i, or any man, can de
clare .... the gifte, wherof
.... vnknowen to my lytell,

power. And this, the same vnknowen
sighe, doth bringe me a newe desyre,
shewinge the good that i haue loste
by my synne, wiche is giuen me a=
gaine, through his grace, and bontie,
wich hath ouercomed all synnes
O my god, what grace, and good
nes is this, wich doth put out so
many synnes. Nowe maye we se
it that thou arte full of all good
loue to make me such an honeste
turne. Alas my god i did not se=
ke the, but i fled, a raune and waye
frome the, and here beneth, thou, thou,
camest to me, with vnwillnes.

but an worme of the earth all na
ked, what do i saye worme? i do
hym wronge, i beynge so naughty
and forsworne full of pride, de=
spite, malice, and treason. The

psal 118   promes wiche my frendes made
when i was baptised, beyng such
allwayes through thy passion to

rom 6 &   fele the mortifieng of my fleshe,
and fol 15 to be allwayes with the in the
cross, where thou hast nayled
(as i do bilieue) and yelded death
deui, and also all synne, wiche
wich i haue often tymes fall in down
agayne, and yet all i haue broken

denied and falsified my promesse
and (through pryde) i did suchewise
lifte vp my wille, that (with sloughte)
my dettie twardes the was forgotten
And the thinge wiche muche more
is, as well the welthe of the promes
that i had of the on the daye of my
baptisme, as also thy loue and pro
messe i haue forgotten all a lizte
What shall i say more: albeit that
often tymes thou witstoudest myn
vnhapynes, geuinge so many war
nitges, by faythe, and sacramentes,
admonishinge me by preachinge,
and also conforting me by the

marke, 10.

receyuinge of thy worthy body and
holy b[...] also promysinge to put
me in the rowe of them that are
in parfaitte innocency but i haue
all these goodnes put in forgetful
nes. Often tymes haue i broken
with the conuenante ffor my poore
soule was to moche fede of with
yll bread and damnable doctrine
i despysinge succoure and phisicke
suche as wolde haue helped me
and if i [had ben] willinge to tolze
for i knowe no man whom i had
required for there is neyther man
sainte or [...] angell for whom thei

harte of a sinner will chaunge. A...
good Iesus, thou seynge my blynd...
and that at my nede i could haue
no succoure of men, than didest ...   actes. 4.
thou opene the waye of my salua
cion. O what goodnes and swittenes
Is there any father to the daugther,
or els brother to the syster, wiche
wolde euer do as he hath done
for he came in to hell for to suc-   1. Ihon. 4
coure my soule where against his
wille she was willinge to perishe
bycause she did not loue the. alas
thou hast loued her. O charitie
seruente and inflammed, thou

art not flalze to loue, thou, wiche
louest euery body, yea, and also

rom.s thye enimyes, not only forgiuinge
them their offences, but also to giue
thyselfe (for their saluacion, libertie
and deliuraunce) to the deathe,
crosse, trauayle, payne, and souf
fring. Whan i do confydere what
is the occasion of thy loue towardes

eph. me, i can se nothinge els but loue
wich inciteth the to geue me this
that i can not deserue. Than (my
god) as ferfourth as i can se, i ought

i timo. to geue no thankes for my salua
cion but onely vnto the, to whom

I owe the prayse for it, as to hym
wich is my sauioure and creatour.
Alas what thinge is this, thou hast
done so muche for me, and yet art
thou not contente to haue forgiuen
me my synnes, but also gyuen
vnto me the right gracious gyfte   ephe. 2
of grace. ffor it shuld suffise me (i
cominge out of suche a daunger)
to be ordred like a straunger: but
thou doest handle my soule (if so
i durst say) as a mother, daugther
syster, and wife. I lord, i wich am
not worthy, for to aske bread, to   take.
come neare the dore of the ryght

highe place, where thy dwellinge is.
O what grace is this that so sodenly
thou vouchesafest to drawe my soul
in suche hignes that she seeth herselfe
the ruler of my body. She poore

philip 4 — ignorance, and layme, doth synde
herselfe with the riche, wise, and strõg

zach. 2 — bycause thou hast written in her harte
and rom. — the rolle, of thy spirite, and holy word

ephe. 2 — geuenge her true fayth to receyue it,
wiche thinge made her to cõceyue
thy sonne, beleuinge hym to be god

rom. — man, sauyoure and also the true
remitter of all sinnes. Therfore
dere thou vouchesafe to assure

the ...... is mother of thy sonne
..... thou art the onely father,
And furthermore (o my father) here
is a greate loue, ffor thou art not
slake of well doynge, sythe that
thy sonne full of diuinite, hath take
the body of a man, and did ioyne   philip.2.
hymselfe with ours. This, wiche thing
a man can not vnderstand, onles
he hath a true fayth. It hath plea
sed the to put hym so neere vs.
that he did ioyne hymself vnto
oure fleshe, than we (seynge hym
to be called man) doo call hym
syster, and brother. Nowe, there

ſaule (wich may ſay of herſelfe, that
ſhe is the ſyſter of god) ought to be
aſſured in her harte. After this doeſt
thou declare with great loue, howe
her creacion is onely the good wille
wich it pleaſyth the to haue alwayes
twardes her: geuyng aſſuraunce ỹ

ephe: i ~ before her firſt daye (prouidine for
her) thou haſt had thy loue in her,
and how (through loue) thou haſt
begotten her, as (alone) thou caneſt
do very well. And alſo how thou
... put her withine this body
nor for life ... withſoughte, but that
both of them ſhuld haue no other

exercise, but onely to thinke howe
to do ~~you~~ some seruice vnto the:
than the truth maketh her to ſee,
that there is true paternite in the.
O what honnoure, what good and
glory hath the soule, wich doth
alwayes remember, that ſhe is thy
daughter: and, in callinge the father,
ſhe doth thy cômaundementes.
What is there more, is that all, no:
it pleaſeth the to gyue her an other
name, to call her thy wife, and
ſhe to call the huſbande, decla-
ringe how thou haſt frely decla-
red the mariage of her. By the

baptisme thou haddest ~~made~~ hast
made a promesse to giue her
goodes, and riches. Thou doest take
her synnes, ffor she hath nothinge
els, the wiche adam her father did
giue her. All her treasures are no
thinge els but synnes, wiche thou

1.peter.2. hast talzen vpon the, and payed
all her whole dette. With thy
goodes, and great laundes, thou
hast made her so riche, and with
so great a ioynter, that she (knowing herselfe to be thy auowed
wife) doth beleue to be quitte of
all that she oweth, estiming very

lytell, this that she doth se here=
neth. She forsaketh her olde father,
and all the goodes that he geueth
for her husbandes sake. Surely (o my
god) my soule is well hurte, to be side
of suche good, for to leaue the plea=
sure of this worlde for the same wich
is euerlasting, where peace is without
warre. I meruaille howe she (for ioye)
doth not lese her witte, cõtenaunce,
and speche. Father, father, alas
what ought i to thinke. shall my
spirite be so bolde to take vpon
him to call the father, ye, and also,
oure father, for so hast thou said

math. 6. in the pater noster. But to call me, a daughter, hast thou ſo ſayd, i beſeche the tell it me. alas ye, ſor (with great ſwittenes) thou ſaydest, *daug-*
prouer. 23. ther, lende me thy harte: O my god, in ſtedde of lending, he is redy to giue hymſelfe wholy vnto the. Receyue hym, than, and do not permitte, that any body put hym ſarre ſrome the: ſo that ſoreuer (with ſaythfull ſtedſaſtenes) he may loue the, with a daugtherly loue. Now my lorde, if thou be my father, may i thinke me to be youre that i am thy mother. ffor i can not

perceyue howe I shuld com[e to]
the, wich hast created me. But [thou]
didest ~~my~~ (satisfie) doutte, when in preachi[ng]
(stretching furth thy handes) thou
didest say: Those that shall do [the will] mat. 12
the wille of my father, they are
my brethern and mother. I beleue
than: that (hearing or reding the
wordes that thou didest [say,] and
hast sayd by thy holy prophettes
the same also, wich (through thy
good preachers) thou do dayly de
clare vnto men: beleuing, and de
bringe stedfastely to fulfille it) that
through loue I haue begotten the[m]

not
hym
reuer
the m[ay]
ly loue
my fa[ther]
oure
can not

Therfor withoute any feare will
i take vpon me the name of thy
mother. Mother of god, o switte
virgin mary. I befeche the be not fory
that i take vp suche a titell: I do
neyther steale, or pretende any
thinge vpon thy priuilege. ffor
thou (onely hast aboue all wome
luke receaued so great honnoure, that
no man can not in hymselfe
comprehende, howe he hath ben
willinge to take in the our fleshe.
ffor thou art mother, and persytt
virgin, before, after, and in hys
byrth. Thou didest beare and

...rished hym in thy holy ... he.
Thou didest folowe hym at iŋ
preaching, and also when he was
troubled. Nowe to speke shorte,
thou hast with god founde the gra luke.1
ce, that oure enmy (through malice
and deceyte) had caused adam, and
hys posterite to lese. Through eue,
and hym, we had loste it and, by   rom.5
thy sonne, hath ben yelded vnto   ihon.1
vs againe. Therfore hast thou ben
ryghtely named, full of grace. ffor luke.1
thou lackest neyther grace or ver
...yth that he (wich is the beste
... them that be good ...

the spring of all goodnes, grace and power, wich hath created in the so pure innocency, that thou art the example of all vertues) hath buylded in the, his dwellinge, and temple He (through loue) did conforme himselfe with the, and thou art transformed with hym. Therfore, if any man shuld thinke to geue the greater prayse than god hymselfe hath done, it were a blasphemy. ffor there is no suche prayse, as the same is wich cometh frome god. Also hast thou had so stedfaste, and constante a fayth, that by grace

she had the power to make the godly. Therfore i wil not take vpon
me to gyue the greater prayse, than
the honnoure wich the souerayne
lorde hath gyuen vnto the. ffor
thou art his corporall mother, and
also (through fayth) his spirituall
mother. Than, i ffolowinge thy faith
with humilitie) am hys spirituall
mother. Alas my god: of the fraternite that thou hast twardes me
through thy humblenes, in callinge
me, syster, didest thou euer sayd
any thinge of it: alas, ye, ffor thou
hast broken the kinrede of myne

marginalia:
ple the
himself
fformed
man
reater
hath
ffor
he same
Also
and

olde father, callinge me, daughter of
adoption. Well, than sjth that we
haue but one father, i wjll n t feare
to call the, my brother. ffor so hast
thou fayd by falomon in his ballet,

Cantic. 4. fayenge, my fyster, thou hast won
ded my harte with the fwitte loke
of one of thy eyes, and with one
of thy heeres. Alas good brother,
I wifhe for nothinge els, but that
in wondinge the, i might fynde my
felf wonded with thy loue. And
~~~~ fe thou doest call me, wife,
fhewinge that thou louest me,
and call me, by true loue

my doue, ryſe vp my ſpowſe. Ther cantic, 2
fore ſhall i ſay, with louing faith.
thou art myn, and i am thyne.

o h ſt   Thou doeſt call me, loue, and faire
     ſpowſe: if ſo it be, ſuche haſt thou
aſt wo made me. Alas; doth it pleaſe the
to geue me ſuche names: they are
hable to breake a mans harte, and
rother. to kindle hym by ſuche loue. When
he thinketh vpon the honnoure
wich is greater than he hath deſer
ued. Mother, mother: but what a
childe is it; it is of ſuche a ſonne, ÿ
my harte doth breake, for loue.
My god, my ſonne: O ieſus what

speche & spelzing is this: mother and
daugther: O hapy kinrede. O what
swittenes doth procede of thesame
paternite. But what daugtherly
loue, and reuerent feare ought i to
haue twardes hym. My father, ye
psal 70. and my creatoure, my protectoure
and, 30. and my conseruatoure: to be thy
syster: alas here is a greate loue.
Nowe doest thou brealze my hart
in the middes: malze rowme for
thesame so swttte a brother; so that
no other name be written in the
but onely my brother, iesus, the
sonne of god. ffor vnto no other

man wil i geue place, for all the
grudginge, and beyttinge y̆ they
can do vnto me. Kepe my harte
than, my brother, and lett not thy
enmy entre in it. O my father, bro
ther, childe, and spowse: with
handes ioyned, humbly vpon my
knees, i yelde the thankes, and
praise, that it pleaseth the to turne
thy face twardes me, conuerting
my hart, and coueringe me with
such grace, that thou doest se
no more my yuels, and synnes
so well hast thou hydden them,
that it semeth thou hast put them

in forgetfulnes, yea, and also they seme to be forgotten of me, wich haue cōmitted them. ffor, faith and loue, causeth me to forgett them, putting wholy my truste in the onely. Than, my father, in whom lyeth vnsayned loue: wherof can i haue feare in my harte: I confesse that i haue done all the yuell that one man can do, and that, of my selfe, i am naught, also that i haue offended the, as the prodigal childe did, folowing the folishe tradde of the fleshe, where i haue spent all my substancy, and also all the

iames, 3.

abundance of goodes, wich i had re-
ceiued of the. ffor, pouertie had
thered me, euen as hey, and yelded
my spirite deed for hunger, selzyng
to eate the reliefz of swinne: but i
founde very lytell sauoure in such
meates Than seyng my liuynge
to be so miserable) did returne
vnto the, O father. Alas i haue sinned   Iohn
in heauen, and before the; I am   luke. 15.
not worthy (i tell it afore euery
man) to call myselfe be called thy
childe, but (o bountiefull father)
do ye worse vnto me, but as to
one of thy housholde seruauntes

Alas what loue, and zeale is thys:
ffor thou woldest not tary my com
ming, and prayer, but (stretching
furth thy hande) receuedyst me:
when i did thinke that thou wol
dest not se me; and in stedde to
haue punishemente, thou doest as
sure me of my saluacion. Where
is he, than, that shall punishe me
when my father shall denye hym
my synne. There is no iudge that
can condemne any man, onlesse
god himselfe wolde damne hym.
I feare not to haue lake of goodes,
syth i haue god for my father.

My enmy shall do me no harme,
ffor my father shall vndowe hys
power. If i owe any thing he shal paye
it for me. If i haue deserued death
he (as a kinge) shall geue me gra
ce, and pardon, and delyuer me
frome prison, and hanging. But
here is the worse: what mother
haue i ben: ffor after that i had
receued the name of a true mother
than haue i ben to rude vnto the.
ffor after that i had conceyued,
and brought the furth; i lefte rea
son, and subiette vnto my owne by the
will, not takinge hede vnto the,

3 king.3. i fell aslepe, and gaue place to my great enmy: the wich in the nyght of ignoraunce (i beyng aslepe) did steale the frome me, craftely, and in the place she did put her childe wich was dead. So did i lese the by my owne faute, wich thinge is a harde remorse for me. Nowe haue i loste the by mine owne fautte, by cause i toke no hyde to kepe the. My enmy, my sensualite (i beyng in my beastely slepe) did steale the frome me, and gaue me an other childe hauinge no life in hym, wich is called synne, whom i will not haue. ffor i do yt

terly forsake hym. She affyrmyd
that he was myn owne, but i
knewe hym to be hers. ffor as soone
as i came to the light of the grace
wich thou haddest geuen me, than
i knewe my glory to be chaunged
when i sawe the deed child not to
be myn: ffor thesame wich was a
liue (whom she had taken awaye)
was mynowne. Betwene Iesus, and
synne, is the chaunge so apparent,
But here is a straunge thing: This
olde woman causeth me to kepe hym wich
is dead, whom she sayeth to be
myn, and so she will maytene. O

Salomon true iudge, thou hast herd
this lamentable proces, and or-
deyned (contenting the parties)
that my child shuld be diuided
in two partes The false woman
agreeth it shuld be so: but i (re-
membring hym to be my owne
sonne) was rather contente to
lese hym, than to se his body par-
ted in two peces (ffor, true, and
parfaitte loue is neuer contente
with one halfe of this that she
lou(th)) but i wolde rather wyppe
for my whole losse, than to reco-
uer but one halfe. My mind shuld

not be satisfied, if i had recouered
one halfe withoute life. Alas geue
her rather the childe wiche is a=
liue: better it is for me to dye, thā
to Ie Iesuschrist dyuided. But (o my
lorde) thou didest loke better to
it, than i, ffor, thou (seynge the
payne that i did suffer, and howe
i did rather forsake my ryghte
than to se suche cruelnes) saydest,
this is the true mother, and cau   3.king.3.
sed them to gyue me my childe
againe. O swytte iesus, haue i
founde the after to haue proued
me, yf i did loue the, i who had

loste the, yet didest thou retourne
vnto me. Alas doest ^thou vouchafe to
come againe to her wiche, beynge
let with synne, coulde not kepe the
O my switte childe, my sonne, my
nourriture, of whom i am ryght
humble creature, do not permytte
that euer i do leaue the; ffor i repent
myselfe of the tyme passed. Nowe
come, my sensualitie, with synnes of
all qualities, ffor thou hast not the
power to make me receyue y̓ childe
wich is dead. The same that i haue
is stronge inough for to defende
me, and he shall not permytte that

thou do take hym awaye frome
me. He is alredy as strong as any
man is: therfore maye i slepe, and
take reste neere of hym. ffor he shal
kepe me better, than i could kepe
hym. Than (as i thinke) i maye //
take reste. O what a swette reste
it is, of the mother, and the sonne
togyther. My swette childe: O my
god; honnoure, and praise be vnto
the, onely, so that euery body maye
perceyue, howe it hath pleased
the, me lesse than nothing to call
a mother: the more that y thing
is straunge, and harde to be done,

the more ought thy goodnes haue
praise for it. And also, i finde myself
more bounde vnto the, than euer i
did, for this that it pleaseth the to
haue reteyned me for thy syster. I
am syster vnto the, but so naughty
a syster, that better it is for me to
hyd suche a name: ffor i fforgettinge
the honnoure, and adoption of so
noble kinrede; also thy so swtte a
brotherly behauoure towardes me
did ryse against the, and (not reme
bring my fauttes, but goynge farre
frome the) did agre with my bro
ther aaron, willinge to giue iudge

mente againste thy worlzes, and also
grudging againste the priuely, wiche
thinge causeth me to haue a great re
morse in my conscience. O bountiefull
god. brother, and true moses, wich
doth all thinges with godnes, and
iustice. i haue estimed thy dedes
to be wiclzed, beynge so bolde, and
sayenge rashely. why hast thou
married a straunge woman: Thou
gyuest vs a lawe, and punishemēt
if we do not fulfille it. and thyselfe
wolde not be bounde to it. forbiding
vs the thinge wich thyselfe dedyst
ffor thou doest forbide vs to

no man; and thou doest kille and
exo. 22. spared none of thre thousande that
thou caused to be slayne. Also god
gaue vs commaundemente by the
that we shuld not marry ÿ daugther of a straunger: but thou tokest
thy wife emonge them. Alas my bro
ther i tolde the a great many of such
wordes, wiche i knowe well to be
folishe, wherof i do repente: for ÿ
truely voyce of god toke me vp
afore i went oute of the place. What
didest thou of my synne: alas my
brother thou woldest not haue
nume. 12 me to be punyshed, but rather

woldest for my helthe, and saluacion, in astzinge for thys great benefite, that it shuld please god to mitigate hys iudgemente: The wiche thinge thou couldest not obtayne; ffor i became a lazare, so that whan any body shulde loke vpon vpon me, might saye that i had not ben wise. And so was i put (like a lazare) frome the tentes and habitacion of the people: ffor a soule can not haue greater punishemente, than to be banyshed frome the company of them that are good, and holy

bycause that a sylze body maye
marre them wiche be in helthe. But
what didest thou ffor seynge my
repentaunce; ffor thou didest helpe
that my penaunce was soone ended
By true loue, thou didest pray for
me, and than did i returne. O
what brother, who in stedde to pu
nishe hys folishe syster wolde
cleaue vnto her. ffor iniury grudge
and greate offence, thou gauest her
grace, and loue in recompense. Alas
my brother this is to moche, thou shul
dest not do suche a good turne vnto
suche a poore woman as i am. I haue

done yll, and thou geuest me good //
for it. I am thine, and thou didest say
that thou art myn. Thyne i am, and
so will i be for euer. I feare no more //
the greut folishenes of aaron. ffor no //
man shall lose me frome the. Nowe
than that we are brother, and syster
togyther, i care but lytell for all other
men. Thy laundes are my owne psal.z
inheritaunce, lett vs than kepe (if it
pleaseth the) but one husholde. Syth
it pleaseth the to humble thyselfe so
moche, as to ioyne thy harte with
myn, in makinge thyselfe a lyuely //
men, i do ryght humbly thanke the

and as for to do it as i ought, it lieth
not in my power. Take my meaning
than, and excuse myne ignoraunce,
syth that i am of so great a kinrede
as to be thy syster: O my god, i haue
good cause to praise, to loue, and to
serue the vnsaynedly and not to de
syre, or feare any thing, but the onely
Kepe me wel, than, ffor i aske no
other brother, or frende. If any mo
ther hath taken any care for her
sonne; If any brother hath hyd the
faute of hys syster: I neuer sawe it,
or elles it was kepte wonders secrette,
that any husbande wolde forgiue

his wife, after that she had offended
hym an'did returne vnto hym.
There be inoughe of them, wiche for
to auenge their wronge, did cause
the iudges to condemne hym [them] to dye.
Other, seynge their wiues synne,
did not soudaynely speare theyr
owne handes to kille them. Other
also (seynge their fauttes to appeare)
did sent them home agayne to
their owne frendes. Other (seynge
their yll dedes, did shutte them in
a prison. Nowe, to spelze shorte,
 vpon all theyr complexions,
 ende of their pretence, is no

thinge els, but punishemente. And ỹ
leße harme that euer i coulde per
ceyue, in punishinge them: thys it
is, that they wolde neuer se them
agayne. ~~shuldest rather.~~ Thou
shuldest rather make the skye to
to turne, than to make the agre
ment betwne the husbande, and
hys wife, whan he knoweth truly
the faulte that she hath done, or
els hath sene, and founde her in
doynge amisse. Wherfore (O my
god) i can finde no man to be cō
pared vnto the: for, thou arte the
parfaicte example of loue, and now

(more than euer i did) i do confesse,
that i haue brotzen myne othe, and
promesse. Alas thou haddest cho
sen me for thy wife. and didest sett   osea. 2.
me vp in great dignitie, and hon
noure (ffor what greatter honour
may one haue than to be in the
place of thy wife, wich swittely ta
keth reste nere to the) of all thy
goodes, quene, maistres, and lady.
and also in suretie, both of body
and soule. i so vile a creature, be
ynge ennoblished by the. Nowe
(to tell the truth) i had more, and
better than any man can desyre

Therfore, my harte hath cause to
syghe alwayes, and with habun-
psal.94. daunce of teares myne eyes to com
out of my head. My mouthe can
not make to many exclamacions
ffor, there is neyther olde, or newe
writtinges, that can shewe so pitiefull a thinge, as thesame is, wiche i
will tell, nowe. Shall, or deare i tell
it, maye i pronounce it withoute
ezech.36. shame: alas ye: ffor, my confusion
is for to shewe the great loue of
my husbande: therfore i care not,
if for his worship, i do declare my
shame. O my sauioure wiche

dyed, and was crucified on the
crosse, for my synnes: thys dede is
not such as to leaue hys sonne, and
as a childe, to offende hys mother:
or elles (as a syster) to grudge, and
chyde agaynst hys brother. Alas
thys is worse: ffor, the offense is the
greater, where more loue, and know
ledge is. And the more we receyue
of ——— familiarite, and benefites the
o—— ——————— deceyue hym
—ich was called spowse, and loued
—the as h— —wne soule. Shall i
— truth y— I haue less forgot
—— unn— ——— from —ho—

I did leaue the, for to go at my pleasure. I haue forsaken the for to
choyce an worse. I did leaue the (o
spring of all goodnes, and faythfull
promesse. I did leaue the: but whether
went i, in a place where nothinge
is but cursydnes. I haue lefte, my
trusty frende, and louer worthy to
be loued aboue all other. I haue
lefte the, through myne owne yll
will. I haue lefte the full beautie, good
nes, wisedom, and power: And (for

deuto. 32. the better to outdrawe myselfe
frome thy loue) i haue taken thyne
enmy, wich is the dyuell, y world

and the fleshe: for whose to ouercome
thou hast foghte so sore on the crosse
for to put me in libertie, whom they   gala. 4.
had a longe tyme kepte prisonnere,
slaue, and so bounde, that no man
coulde cause me to humble myselfe
And, as for the loue, and charitie, y
ishuld haue towardes the: they did
quenshe it; so that the name of iesus
my husbande (wich before i had to
founde so switte) was to me, tedious.   prouer. 1
and i did hate it, so that oftentimes
i did ceaste at it. And if any man
(we hearinge a sermon) shuld saye
vnto me, the preacher sayeth well

i wil answere, it is true: but my w
wordes ~~doth flee~~ did flee awaye, as
a fether doth. and i went neuer to
the church but for maner salze.
all my dedes were but ypocrisy: for
my mynde was in other places.
I was enoyed when i herde spealze
of the: for, ~~my mynde was in~~
~~other places~~ i was more willinge
to go at my pleasure. Nowe to
spelze shorte, all this that thou di
dest forbide me, i did it and all y
thou cōmaundedest me to do: I
did eschue it, and all thys(O my
god)bycause i did not loue the

et for all thys that i did hate for
falze, raune awaye, and betrayed
he bycause i shuld geue thy place
to an other: hast thou suffered y
shuld be mod molzed, or elles bea
ten, or lzilled: Hath thou sett me
out me in darlze prison, or bani
shed syttyng nought by me.
Hast thou talzen awaye agayne
thy gyftes, and iouyelles, for to pu
nishe me of my vnfaythful
sinnes. Haue i loste my iointer
wich thou hadyst promysed me
bycause i did offende against the
Am i accused by the afore

iudge, as a naughty woman shuld
be, yet hast thou forbiden me, that
i shuld neuer presente myselfe be
fore the (euen as reason was) and
also that i shuld neuer come to thy
house. O true parsaitte husbande
and frende, the moste louinge
emonge all good louers. Alas
thou hast done otherwise: ffor
thou soughtest for me ~~diligentely~~
when i was goynge in the most
depe place of hell, where all the
~~geoes~~ yueles are done. I that
was so farre frome the, ~~both~~ hart
and mynde oute of the true way

luke 15
and 18

than didest thou call vpon me say
enge. My daughter: harkze, and se psal. 47
and bowe thy hearinge towardes
me. Forget, also, thesame maner of
people, with whom thou didest ro
raunc awaye frome me, and also
the house of thyne olde father, where
thou hast dwelled so longe: than
the kinge full of godlines shal desyre
thy company. But, when thou sawest
that thys swittte, and gracciouse spe
kzing, did me no good: than thou
begannest to cry. Come vnto me math. 11
all ye wich are werey with laboure.
I am i that shall receyue, and set

you with my bread. Alas i wolde
not vnto all these wordes: ffor i dou
^harke
ted whether it were thou, or els a
symple writtinge, that so sayd. ffor i
was so folishe that without loue i
did rede your worde, I sawe, and
^thy
vnderstoude well that the compa
rayfons of the vineyarde, wich brou
brought furth thornes, and poy
fons in stedde of good fruite; thou
saydest all this of me wich had so
done Consideringe also that when
^call
thou didest the wife, sayenge, come
come agai[n]   all this thou didest
spe[a]ke bycause   ... my synne leaue

deuto. 32
esay. 5

and of all these wordes, i did as
though i had vnderstand neuer
a worde. But when i did rede ie
remy the prophet, i confesse that
i had in the reading of it, feare
in my harte, and shame in my
face. I will tell it, ye, and with y
teares in myne eyes, and all for thy
honnoure, and to supresse my
pride. Thou hast sayd this by
thy holy prophet. If a woman
hath offended her husbande, and
leste hym for to go with a other
man: they neuer sawe that the hus
bande wolde talze her againe. Ie

she not estimed to be polluted, and of no
value. The lawe doth consente to put
her in the handes of the iustice, or els
dryue her a waye, and neuer se her, or
take her againe. But thou, wich hast
made separacion of my beade, and
did put thy false louers in my place,
and commyted fornicacion with
them: yet for all thys thou mayest
come vnto me againe ffor i will
not be angry against the. Lifte vp
thyne eyes, and loke vp than shalt
thou se in what place thy synne had
leade the. and how thou lyest down
in the earth. O poore soule, loke where

thy synne hath put the: euen vpon the
hyghe wayes, where thou didest wayte.
and taryed for to begyle them that //
came by. Euen as a thief doth wich
is hydden in wildernes. Therfore (ha
uinge fullfilled thy pleasure) thou hast
infected (with fornicacion) all the so
earth wiche was aboute the. Thyne eye
thy forehed and thy face, had loste
all their good maner. ffor they were
suche as those of an harlotte, and //
yet thou haddest no shame of thy //
synne. And the surplus that ieremy
sayeth. Wich thinges constrayneth //
me to know my wretched life and

to wishe (with sorowfull syghes) the
daye, the houre, the moneth, the yere
and the tyme, that i did leaue the
yeldinge myselfe condemned, and
worthy to be for euer in the euerla
stinge fyre. The same feare (wiche
prouer. 15. doth not procede of me, but come
of the, and excedeth all pleasure)
had almoste put me in despayre,
as often as i did remember my
synne: yf it hath not ~~~~~ thou
neuer leftest me. ffor as foone as
thou knewest my wille bowen so
to obey the: than (puttinge in me
aluely fayth) thou didest vse of thy

:lemency, and goodnes, so that after i
knewe the, to be lord, maister, and
kinge (of whom i ought to haue feard)
han founde i my feare to be quenshed
)eleuinge that thou were so gracious
good, swytte, and pitiefull husbande,
       shuld
hat i (wich rather hyd me, than to
                          d
he we myselfe) was not a feare to go
and seke for the: and in sekinge i
founde the. But, what didest thou,
than; hast thou refused me: Alas (my
god) no, but rather excused me. se
Hast thou turned thy face from me.
no. for, thy swytte loke hath pene-
tred my harte, wonding hym

death, geuinge me remorse of my
synnes. Thou hast not put me back
with thy hande: but with both thy
armes, and with a swifte and man
ly harte, thou didest mete with me
by the waye: and not reprochinge
my fauttes, embraſſedſt me. I could
not se, beholding thy contenance,
that euer thou didest perceyue
myne offence. ffor, thou hast done
as moche for me, as though i had
ben good, and honeste, and didest
hyd my fautte from euery body
in geuing me againe the parte of
thy hedde, and also shewinge that

luke.15.

the multitude of my synnes are so
hydden, and ouercome by thy
great victory, that thou wilt neuer
remember them; so thou seist nothig
in me but, the grace, gystes, and ver
tues, wich it pleaseth thy goodnes
to gyue me. O charitie: ise well y
thy goodnes doth consume my le
udnes, and maketh me a godly
and beautifull creature. Thys that
was myn thou hast destroyed it
and made me so parfaitte a creature
that thou hast done me as muche
good, as any husband can do vnto
hys wife. geuenge me a faythfull

hope in thy promesses. Nowe i
haue (through thy good grace) reco
uered the place of thy husbande
wife. O hapy, and desyred place,
gracious bedde, trone ryght hono
rable, seate of peace, rest of all
warre, hygh steppe of honnoure,
seperate from the earth: doest thou rece
thys vnworthy creature, gyuinge
her the sceptre, and crowne of
thyne empire, and glorious realme
Who did euer heare speke of such
a thinge; as to rayse vp one so high
wich of herselfe was nothing, and
maketh of a great value, thys ỹ

of it selfe was naught Alas what thing
is thys. ffor, i casting myne eyes an
high, i se in the goodnes so vnknowen
grace, and loue so incomprehensible
that my syght is lefte inuisible Thā
am i constrayned to loke down://
and lokzing down, i do se what i
am, and what i was willinge to be
Alas i do se in it the leudnes, darke
nes and extreme depenes of my
yuelles. Also my death, wiche by
humblenes closeth myne eye. The //
admyrable goodnes of thē, and ỹ
vnspekeable yuell wich is in me.//
Thy hignesse, and right pure maieste

my ryht fragile, and mortall nature.
Thy gyftes, gooddes, and beatitude,
my malice, and great vnkidnes.
Howe good thou art vnto me; and
howe vnkind i am vnto the. Thys
that thou wilt: and this that i pur
shue. Wich thinges considered, cau
seth me to meruayle, how it plea
seth the to ioyne thy selfe vnto me,
seynge that there is no comparaysō
betwene vs both: ffor thou arte
my god, and i am of thy worke
Thou arte my creatore, and i am
thy creature. Nowe, to speke shorte,
i can not define what it is of the

ffor i knowe myselfe to be the lest
thinge that can be compared vnto
the. O loue, thou madest thys a-
grement, when thou didest ioyne
life, and death togyther. but theis
vnion hath viuified death. Life dy-
enge, and life without ende, hath
made oure death a life. death hath
geuen vnto life, quycke death.
Through such death (i beyng deed)
receyued life: and by death, i am
rauished with hym wich is aliue.
I liue in the, and, as for me, i am
deed. ffor. death is nothinge els to
me, but the cominge oute of a prison

Death is life vnto ffor through &
death i am aliue. This mortall life
yeldeth me full of care, and sorowe:
and death yeldeth me contente.
O what a goodly thinge it is, to
dye, wich causeth my soule to liue
in delyuringe her, trough thys mor
tall death, exempt from miserable
death, and equall vnto god, with
so mighty a loue, that (onles she
doth dye) she languisheth alwayes
Is not than, the soule blameles wich
wold fine dye, for to haue such
life ye surely ffor she ought to
call the death her welbeloued

philip. r.

frende. O swittc death, pleasaunte
sorowe, mighty keye, delyuringe
from sorowe, all those, wich tru//
stinge in the, and in thy passion //
were mortified, bycause the did truste
in the, and in thy death. ffor with
an switte slepe, thou didest putt //
them frome the death, wich caused
them to lamente. O how hapy is //
the same deedly slepe vnto hym, the
wiche when he waketh, doth finde
(through thy death) the euerlasting
life. ffor the death is no other thing
to a christen man, but a libertie //
frome his mortall baunde. And,

the death wich is fearefull to ye wiked
is pleasante, and agreabie to them y^t
philip be good. Than is death (through
hebre.2 thy death destroyed. Therfore my
god, if i were rightely thaught, i
shuld call the death, life, ende of
laboure and begyning of euerlastig
ioye. ffor i knowe that the longe
life doth lett me frome thy syght
O death, come, and breake the sam
obstacle of life, or els loue do nowe
a miracle. Syth that i can not yet
se my spowse: transforme me with
hym, both body and soule: and
than shall i the better tary for y^e

cominge of death. lett me dye, that
i maye liue with hym: for there is
none, that can helpe me, onles it be
thou onely. O my sauioure, through
fayth, i am plaunted, and ioyned   rom. 11
with the. O what vnion is thys.//
syth (through fayth) i am sure of //
the; and nowe i maye call the: 1hon. 1.
sonne, father, spowse, and brother
Father, brother, sonne, husband
O what giftes thou doest gyue. //
by the goodnes of those names. //
O my father: what paternite. O
my brother: what fraternite. O //
my childe: what dilection. O my

husband. O what conionction.//
Father full of humilitie. Brother//
hauinge taken our similitude. Sōne
engendred through faith, and cha
ritie. husbande louing in all extre
mite. But whom doest thou loue
Alas it is she, the wich thou hast //
withdrawen frome the snare.//
wherein, through mlice, she was
bounden. and gaue her y̑ place
name, and office, of a daughter,
syster, mother, and wyfe. O my sa
uioure: thesam swittenes is of great//
fauoure, right pleasaunte, and of //
a swite tast. y̑ any may speke

vnto the, or els heare the. And cal
linge the (withoute any feare) father
childe, and spowse: hearing the, hiere, 3
i do heare myselfe to be called,
mother, syster, daughter, and spo cantic, 4.5
spowse. Alas, nowe may e̊ y soule
(wich doth finde suche swittenes) to
be consumed by loue. Is there any
loue that may be compared vnto
this, but it hath some yuell condi
cion. Is there any pleasure to be //
estimed. Is there any honnoure, //
but it is accounted for shame. Is //
there any profitte to be compared
vnto this. i lowe to speke shorte. //

is there any thinge. that more I
could loue; alas no: ffor. he y̆ loueth
god. doth repute all these thinges
philip. 3. worse than a donge hyll. Plesure
profitte. and honnoure of thys
worlde are but trifles vnto hym
wich hath founde the loue of
god. ffor suche loue is so profita
ble, honorable, and abundante:
psal. 106. that, she onely, contenteth y̆ harte
and yeldeth hym so contente (as i
deare saye) that he neuer desyreth
or wolde haue other thinge. ffor
whosoeuer hath god (as we
ought to haue hym) he that asketh

any other thinge, is a superfluous //
man. Nowe, thanked be god, throug
faith, haue i recouered, and gotten //
the sam loue: w therfore i ought to
be satisfied, and contente. Nowe i //
haue the, my father, for the defence
of the folishenes of my longe youth
Nowe haue i the, my brother, for to
fuccoure my forowes, wherin i find
no ende. Nowe i haue the, my fone,
for the onely stey of my feble age. //
Nowe haue i the true, and fayth //
full husband, for the satisficing of //
my whole harte, and mynd. Now
syth that i haue the, do forsake //

CPSIA information can be obtained at www.ICGtesting.com
Printed in the USA
BVOW01s0959030816
457659BV00020B/84/P